HISPANIC CULTURE

BY CHRISTY STEELE

Rourke
Publishing LLC
Vero Beach, Florida 32964

Developed by Nancy Hall, Inc., for Rourke Publishing.
© 2006 Nancy Hall, Inc.

Acknowledgments are listed on page 48.

www.rourkepublishing.com

Photo research by L. C. Casterline
Design by Atif Toor and Iram Khandwala

Library of Congress Cataloging-In-Publication Data

Steele, Christy, 1970-
  Hispanic culture / by Christy Steele.
      p. cm. -- (Discovering the arts)
  Includes bibliographical references and index.
  ISBN 1-59515-520-1 (hardcover)
  1. Hispanic American arts--Juvenile literature. I. Title. II. Series.
  NX512.3.H57S74 2006
  704.03'68073--dc22
                        2005010732

Title page: Old Spanish Mission Church at Taos Pueblo, New Mexico.
Priests often traveled with explorers, urging native peoples to become Catholic
and having them build churches.

Printed in the USA
10 9 8 7 6 5 4 3 2 1

CONTENTS

NEW SPAIN

In 1492, Christopher Columbus sailed west across the Atlantic in search of a water route to Asia. Instead, he discovered a world unknown to Europe. Columbus was Italian, but he claimed the lands he found for Spain, the country that had paid for his voyage.

Art and culture in the United States owes much of its richness to **Hispanic** traditions. For about 300 years, the Spanish controlled the American Southwest and Florida. They shaped the art, music, buildings, lifestyle, and dress of the people who lived there.

The Spanish were the first Europeans to settle the West Indies, Mexico, Central America, and parts of South America. They also founded Saint Augustine, Florida, the first colony in the United States. Long before the first British colonists landed in Virginia, the Spanish colonists in New Spain had built cathedrals and universities. They had printing presses and a rich tradition of painting.

Portrait of Montezuma (detail), between 1680 and 1697, attributed to Antonio Rodríguez.

Hernán Cortés and his army arrived in what is now Mexico in 1519. There he learned of the rich Aztec civilization. Their king, Montezuma, sent messengers with gifts of gold and jewelry. The Spanish showed off their horses and guns, which the Aztecs had never seen before. The messengers returned and told Montezuma what they had seen. He wondered whether Cortés was really the serpent god Quetzalcoatl coming to claim his kingdom. Cortés was not a god, but he did conquer the Aztecs and claim Montezuma's kingdom for Spain.

The first colonists in New Spain brought their favorite clothes, books, art, and furniture. They spoke Spanish, dressed in Spanish fashions, and performed Spanish music. They built Spanish-style houses and churches. As colonists and native peoples began to marry and have children, they created art, music, festivals, and stories that blended Hispanic and native traditions. The work of these early artists influences much of the art created by today's Hispanic Americans.

CHAPTER 1

THE ARTS OF NEW SPAIN

More than 450 tail feathers from quetzal birds were used to decorate this headdress, which is said to have belonged to Montezuma.

Before the Spanish arrived, the Aztecs had created feather mosaics and headdresses and carved stone calendars, statues, masks, and jewelry. The Spanish destroyed most of the Aztec artwork because it was not Christian. Still, they could see how talented the Aztecs were. At **mission** schools, native artists were trained to create art that was acceptable to the church. Some of them made beautiful images out of feathers from hummingbirds, parrots, and other birds. Many of the feathers were iridescent and changed color when looked at from different angles.

In the 1500s, painting was considered a trade, and Spanish painters worked under a **guild** system. Beginners served as **apprentices**, working with a master artist for several years. Once they had mastered their trade, they could sign their paintings and work on their own.

In 1557, artists formed the first painters' guild in Mexico City. Indians could belong, but Spanish artists got the best jobs. Many of them formed partnerships and set up family workshops. Often, artists who worked together painted in the same style. Most Indian artists worked in Spanish workshops.

New Spain's painters often depended on prints of artworks brought from Europe. Some of them copied the pictures, while others simply borrowed ideas from them.

Maria, 1590–1600, by Iuanis Cuiris. This feather painting of a weeping Virgin Mary may have been inspired by an engraving made in Rome, Italy.

In 1536, Álvar Núñez Cabeza de Vaca arrived in Mexico City. The story of his adventures, traveling from Florida through Texas, sparked interest in the north. Fray Marcos de Niza was sent to explore what is now New Mexico. He returned with tales of the seven golden cities of Cíbola. Francisco Vasquez de Coronado set out to find them in 1540. While Coronado searched without success for gold in what is now the American Southwest, the artist Cristóbal de Quesada drew maps and painted the people, animals, and landscapes. Unfortunately, no known works of Quesada survive today. The illustration above is a reproduction of an 1897 drawing by Frederic Remington.

The Guardian Angel, before 1639, by Luis Juárez. Juárez painted in the style of Spanish artists, such as Baltásar de Echave Orio, who had moved to Mexico in the 1500s.

In 1566, Simón Pereyns, a master of sculpture and portrait painting, arrived in Mexico. He'd been born in the Netherlands, which was then ruled by Spain. Pereyns was often hired to create **retablos**, or altar screens. These were large frameworks overlaid with gold and filled with religious paintings and sculptures. Pereyns created one of the most famous *retablos* of the late 1500s for San Miguel, a mission church in Huejotzingo.

Pereyns sometimes worked with Andrés de la Concha to complete large *retablo* projects. De la Concha came to Mexico from Seville, Spain, in 1568. An architect, gilder, sculptor, and painter, he was best known for his religious art.

Baltásar de Echave Orio was born in Spain in 1558 and came to Mexico City in 1582. Some people think he received art lessons from his wife, Isabel de Ibia. Orio often painted family crests and portraits for government officials, which helped make him a leader in the art community. In 1609, Orio started the first art school for Spanish people born in New Spain. He also headed the first major New World family of painters, who were active for at least three generations.

In 1565, the Spanish conquered the Philippines. They set up a trade route that stretched across the Pacific Ocean to Acapulco, overland to the Atlantic

Festival in an Indian Village, 1650–1700, by an unknown artist. Many homes in New Spain had one large inside space instead of separate rooms. Those who could afford them often used folding screens to divide up the space.

Ocean, and across the Atlantic to Spain. Some of the trade goods from Asia stayed in New Spain. Among these were Chinese porcelain (china) and Japanese folding screens. Hispanic craftsmen created pottery called **majolica**, whose blue-and-white designs imitated the more expensive porcelain. Some of the artists painted or carved their own large folding screens.

Born in a small village outside Mexico City, Juana de Asbaje could read at age three. By the time she was seven, she was writing verse. In 1669, she became a nun and took the name Sor Juana Inés de la Cruz. Sor Juana continued to write poems and plays. Her work was published, and she was considered the best poet of her time. Church authorities, however, did not approve. In 1694, they forced her to stop writing and give up her library. Sor Juana died the following year.

Portrait of Sor Juana Inés de la Cruz, 1750, by Miguel Cabrera

CHURCHES & MISSIONS

Spain was a Roman Catholic country, and so was New Spain. Aztecs and other native peoples were forced to give up their beliefs and become Roman Catholics. They were then put to work building churches and missions.

In Mexico City and other large towns, the churches were usually made of stone. Often, they were decorated inside and out. Priests hired artists to make statues of religious figures and paintings. Some artists made paint by mixing colored powders with water, then painted large pictures called **frescoes** on wet plaster walls.

The Metropolitan Cathedral in Mexico City is the oldest church in the Americas. Begun in 1562, the cathedral was not completed until 1813. The building is a showcase of the styles that were popular during all those years, from **baroque**—a style defined by highly detailed decoration—to classical, a simpler style that looked back to ancient Greece and Rome.

Some priests traveled with Spanish explorers to frontier areas of New Spain. Along the way, they built large church complexes called missions. These served as centers of Spanish

The Metropolitan Cathedral in Mexico City was built on the site of an Aztec temple destroyed by Hernán Cortés.

colonial control. Each mission had a courtyard surrounded by a church, living quarters, and stables. A wall usually encircled all the buildings.

Most mission churches were made of **adobe**, a mixture of straw and clay. Native people had always built up adobe walls as they went, shaping them by hand. The Spanish introduced the art of building with adobe bricks. After the bricks were formed, they were left to harden in the sun. This allowed the buildings to go up much faster.

A carved framework covered with gold leaf surrounds the paintings and statues of saints in the *retablo* of the Santo Domingo church in Oaxaca, Mexico.

In some missions, such as this one in Taos, New Mexico, bells sat in specially cut holes in the wall. Priests rang the bells to call people to church services.

Portrait of an Indian Noblewoman: Sebastiana Inés Josefa de San Agustín, 1757, by an unknown artist. The caption on this portrait gives the sitter's name and age (16) as well as the names of her parents. Sebastiana's clothing and jewelry combine elements of native and Spanish fashion.

As more native-born artists learned to paint, they began to create their own style. Their paintings were realistic and were known for their rich colors, especially blues and reds. This style of painting is called Mexican baroque.

Wealthy people paid artists to paint portraits of their family members. To pose, they dressed in their best clothes and wore expensive jewelry to show off their wealth. Portraits in New Spain often included an **inscription**, or caption, that gave the name of the sitter and other information about him or her.

By the 1700s, many racial groups lived in New Spain and many intermarried. Often, a person's status and wealth depended on which **caste**, or group, he or she belonged to. At one time, there were 16 castes. For example, the ruling *Criollos*, or Creoles, were Spanish people born in New Spain. People of Spanish and Indian descent were called *mestizos*, and those of mixed African-American and Spanish ancestry were called *mulattoes*. To record the social order, artists created paintings called *castas*. Most *casta* paintings are a series of 16 scenes, each showing a family and their offspring. The first image is of the pure Creole family. The second might feature a *mestizo* family, and so on.

The more racially mixed a family, the lower they stood on the social ladder.

Enconchados were an art form developed in Mexico City in the mid- to late 1700s. These pictures combined painting with mother-of-pearl insets. This style may have been inspired by Japanese mother-of-pearl works or by pre-Hispanic mosaics that used shells and stones to make a picture.

Casta painting, 1700s, by an unknown artist.
This painting illustrates three castes: The father is *alvarazado* (mixed Spanish, African, and Indian for several generations), the mother is mulatto, and their child is *borquino*.

Between 1787 and 1803, Martin de Sessé y Lacasta and José Mariano Mociño set out from New Spain with a group of explorers. They traveled south to Central America and as far north as Alaska. With them were several artists who drew the plants and animals they saw. Altogether, they made about 1,800 drawings. After Mociño died in 1820, the drawings were thought to be lost. Then, in 1980, they turned up in the library of a family in Barcelona, Spain. Today, the drawings are housed at Carnegie Mellon University in Pittsburgh, Pennsylvania.

CHAPTER 2

COLONIAL
ARTS AND CRAFTS

This wool-on-wool *colcha* embroidery was made in New Mexico during the late 1700s to 1800s.

In 1598, Juan de Oñate started the first Spanish colony in what is now New Mexico near Santa Fe. To create a trade route to its northern colony, the Spanish expanded the early trails of native peoples. The royal road, or El Camino Real, was an 1,800-mile- (2,900-km-) long trail that stretched from Mexico City to Santa Fe. In the early 1600s, priests built a few missions in Arizona. The first Spanish missions reached Texas in 1682 and California by the mid-1700s.

Women from the southwestern Pueblo and Navajo tribes had been master weavers long before the Spanish arrived. They wove fine cotton cloth on looms to create blankets and clothing. The Spanish colonists had also practiced weaving, but they wove wool from the sheep they'd brought with them from Spain. The colonists who went north with Oñate took several thousand sheep as well as horses and cattle. By 1800, both Hispanics and Native Americans were weaving with wool.

Hispanic weavers blended Spanish and native patterns. Their weavings often sported zigzag or checkerboard patterns. Sometimes they were woven with stripes. The weavers used natural vegetable dyes to color the wool, creating bright blue, red, and yellow colors. Master weavers wove diamonds, stars, flowers, and animal shapes into their fabric.

The word **colcha** means "bed covering," but it also means the kind of stitch used in *colcha* embroidery. Wool-on-wool *colcha* embroidery, called *sabanilla labrada*, was first made in New Mexico. These *colchas* were decorated with birds, animals, flowers, and religious images. Churches sometimes used them to cover their altars.

Because so many Hispanic weavers lived in the Rio Grande valley of New Mexico, their blankets were named "Rio Grande blankets."

Born in Spain, Junípero Serra moved to Mexico to be a missionary when he was 36 years old. In 1767, the church put Serra in charge of building missions in California. He lived and worked among California's Native Americans for the rest of his life. By 1823, the Spanish built 21 missions along 650 miles (1,046 km) of the coast, each a day's walk apart along California's own El Camino Real.

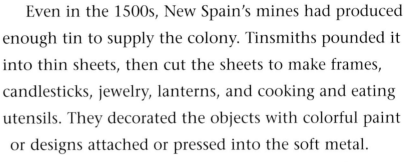

Even in the 1500s, New Spain's mines had produced enough tin to supply the colony. Tinsmiths pounded it into thin sheets, then cut the sheets to make frames, candlesticks, jewelry, lanterns, and cooking and eating utensils. They decorated the objects with colorful paint or designs attached or pressed into the soft metal.

One of the most famous Hispanic tinsmiths was José María Apodaca. He was born in Mexico but moved to Santa Fe as a teenager. In the mid-1800s, he made many frames decorated with starbursts. He often attached ribbon-like pieces of tin to his frames. Sometimes he cut petal-shaped pieces and attached several of them on top of each other so they looked like a rose rising from the tin.

Spanish colonists brought the art of **marquetry**, designs inlaid or glued onto wood, to New Spain in the 1500s. At first, artists used European pattern books to create designs of ivory or different colored woods to decorate crosses, boxes, frames, and furniture. By the 1600s, artists were creating their own patterns using both Spanish and native images. A new Hispanic marquetry style using corn husks and wheat straw was used in New Spain by the late 1700s. It quickly spread north to Spanish New Mexico, where artists began using straw.

To create straw marquetry designs, artists first stained the wooden object to be decorated dark brown or black. Then, they carefully cut pieces of straw to form shapes and patterns. Finally, they attached the straw to the wood.

The dark backgrounds of straw marquetry works make the golden designs show up well.

Throughout New Spain, most Catholic homes had a family altar with **bultos** (also called *santos*), small, brightly colored statues of their favorite saints. Depending on its size, a town might have one or more **santeros**, artists who created these religious images. They carved the *bultos* out of wood, usually leaving the features rough and doll-like. Many *bultos* included a cross or other object important to the saint's story. Shown at left is a *bulto* of San Juan Bautista (Saint John the Baptist).

ART OF THE DEAD

Long before the Spanish arrived, the Aztecs had celebrated the Festival of the Dead. It took place in the Aztec month of Miccailhuitontli, about the last week of July through the middle of August. During the festival, people wore masks and performed dances in honor of their dead relatives. They also displayed skulls, which stood for death and rebirth.

The Roman Catholic Spanish outlawed Aztec religious celebrations, but many native people refused to stop. Finally, the priests moved the dates of the festival to November 1 and 2, when Catholics celebrated All Saints' Day and All Souls' Day. They hoped that over time the Festival of the Dead would be forgotten, but it was not.

Today, the Days of the Dead are still celebrated. Some Hispanics have family altars, where they light candles and place pictures of their dead loved ones and offerings of food and flowers. Some families also decorate the graves of their

This Aztec skull mask has a flint knife for a nose and stone and shell eyes. The holes at the top of the forehead may have held feathers. The mask is probably meant to be an image of Mictantecuhtli, the Aztec god of the dead.

José Guadalupe Posada created many illustrations of *calaveras* and *calacas*. This one was published in 1907.

relatives with candles, gifts, and marigolds, which are the flowers that stand for death. They may even hold picnics at the cemetery. Hispanic artists create special art for the Days of the Dead. The most popular artworks are **calaveras** and **calacas**. These are pictures or sculptures of skulls and skeletons. Also common are skull masks, coffins, and bones. Many Hispanic communities have parades and dances where people wear skull masks or dress as skeletons.

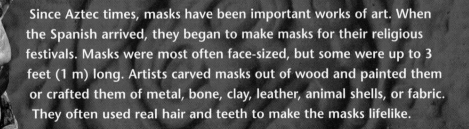

Since Aztec times, masks have been important works of art. When the Spanish arrived, they began to make masks for their religious festivals. Masks were most often face-sized, but some were up to 3 feet (1 m) long. Artists carved masks out of wood and painted them or crafted them of metal, bone, clay, leather, animal shells, or fabric. They often used real hair and teeth to make the masks lifelike.

CHAPTER 3

REVOLUTION

By the early 1800s, Hispanic colonists in New Spain wanted freedom. For 300 years, they had lived by Spanish rules, which limited trade and made them pay heavy taxes. The colonists had seen the United States gain its freedom from England. Now, they, too, wanted their own country.

In 1810, a group of Creoles from Querétaro were plotting to overthrow the Spanish. Instead of going to war, they hoped to talk the Spanish army officers into joining the movement for independence. The government heard about their plan and decided to arrest the Creole leaders. One of them was Miguel Hidalgo y Costilla, a priest from the town of Dolores.

When Hidalgo found out, he rang the church bells as if to call the Indians and *mestizos* to services. When they had gathered, he urged them to rebel against Spain. This speech became known as *El Grito*

Miguel Hidalgo y Costilla, by A. Serrano. Every September 16—the day Hidalgo made his speech calling for rebellion—people all over Mexico shout out, *"Mexicanos, viva Mexico!"* ("Mexicans, long live Mexico!").

Valley of Mexico Seen from the Heights of Tacubaya, by José María Velasco. Velasco often painted the natural beauty of the Valley of Mexico.

de Dolores, or "the cry of pain." The next day, Hidalgo and an army of several hundred marched toward Mexico City. They were forced to retreat, but by November 20, the Mexican Revolutionary War had begun. Today, Hidalgo is called the Father of Mexico.

During the war, artists were hired to travel through parts of northern Mexico that were not settled. They drew maps and painted the animals, plants, and people they saw. Military leaders used some of the artwork to make battle plans.

The colonists finally won their freedom from Spain in 1821 and named their new country Mexico. At that time, Mexico included California, Texas, New Mexico, Nevada, Utah, and parts of Wyoming and Colorado.

José María Velasco was an early Mexican artist. Velasco traveled throughout the country to create his many landscape paintings. His work won first place at an exhibition in Paris, France. He also taught many other artists, including Diego Rivera, how to paint at the Art Academy of San Carlos in Mexico City.

Antonio López de Santa Anna, by an unknown artist. There were 36 changes in the presidency of Mexico between 1833 and 1855, with Santa Anna serving as president 11 times.

During the 1830s, settlers from the United States began moving to present-day Texas, California, and other areas of the Southwest. Soon there were more American settlers than Mexicans, especially in Texas. In 1835, the American Texans declared independence from Mexico, starting the Texas Revolution.

On February 23, 1836, about 1,800 Mexican soldiers led by Antonio López de Santa Anna surrounded the San Antonio de Valero Mission, known today as the Alamo. Santa Anna bombarded the mission with cannonballs for 12 days. On March 6, he attacked. The 200 or so American defenders fought fiercely but the Alamo fell. All the fighters, including Davy Crockett and Sam Bowie, were killed. Just over a month later, the Americans won the war.

The Republic of Texas was an independent country for almost ten years before becoming a state in 1845. Mexico, however, had never accepted Texan independence. After several efforts to settle the matter failed, the United States declared war in May 1846. The Mexican-American War ended less than two years later. Under the Treaty of Guadelupe Hidalgo, the United States took control of about half of Mexico's land. The Rio Grande River now marked the new border between the two countries.

This photograph of a vaquero wearing his fanciest clothes was taken about 1890.

Before there were cowboys, there were Mexican **vaqueros**, or cowhands. Many cowboy customs came from the vaqueros. Vaqueros used a *lazo*, or lasso, to rope cattle. They wore wide-brimmed hats to keep the sun out of their eyes. To protect their legs, they wore heavy sheepskin pants without a seat, known as chaps. Vaqueros held the first rodeos. Twice each year, they gathered to round up the cattle. They branded new calves and separated the cattle into herds. At night, they sang story songs called **corridos**, played card games, and held riding and roping contests.

Joseph Jacinto Mora was just a year old when his parents moved to the United States from Uruguay. He studied art in New York City and worked in Boston before moving west in the early 1900s. Among his many talents, Mora could write, paint, and sculpt. His work includes images of vaqueros, cowboys, and Native Americans. He also created picture maps of California, the Grand Canyon, and other parts of the West.

Five hundred steers there were, all big and quick;
and thirty Americans couldn't keep them bunched together.
Then five Mexicans arrived, all of them wearing good chaps,
and in less than a quarter-hour, they had the steers penned up.

— From "El corrido de Kiansis" ("The Ballad of Kansas")

In the mid-1800s, the story songs called *corridos* first became popular in Mexico and the American Southwest. Singers, or *corridistas*, traveled from town to town performing them. Most *corridos* had three parts. First, the *corridista* greeted the audience and described the story. Then he or she sang the song or poem. The *corrido* ended with the moral of the story and the singer saying goodbye to the audience.

With no radio or television, people used *corridos* to pass on stories, news, and information. Even people who could not read could listen to and remember the songs. The words to *corridos* were often printed on pieces of paper called **broadsides**, which were sometimes illustrated.

José Guadalupe Posada created the illustration for "Corrido de la Cucaracha," which was published in 1915. *Cucaracha* means "cockroach," but during the Mexican Revolution, it was used for women who traveled with their husbands. The *corrido* tells about the hardships of camp life, such as no soap, starch, or ironed clothes.

Francesco "Pancho" Villa and Emiliano Zapata, two heroes of the Mexican Revolution, sit front and center in this photograph of revolutionaries taken in 1911.

After performing, *corridistas* sold the broadsides, which were so cheap that almost anyone could afford them.

José Guadalupe Posada of Mexico City was known as the father of Mexican printmaking. During his life, he drew thousands of illustrations. Many were for *corridos*, but he also drew pictures about history and religion, as well as thrillers. His images of *calaveras* and cartoons poking fun at famous leaders made him popular among the common people.

Posada's broadsides were especially important during the beginning of the Mexican Revolution. Mexicans were unhappy with their government, which controlled all the land, wealth, and power. Many wanted democracy, so common people could vote and influence laws. Posada's art encouraged freedom and revolution.

The revolution started in 1910 and lasted until 1920. During this time thousands of Mexicans moved to California. Hispanics from Mexico become the largest group of immigrants in Los Angeles, numbering close to 250,000 by 1940.

CHAPTER 4

HARD TIMES, WAR, AND NEW BEGINNINGS

Frida Kahlo and Diego Rivera in 1932

After the Great Depression began in 1929, millions of people lost their jobs. President Franklin Delano Roosevelt started government programs to help. From 1935 to 1942, some Hispanic artists found jobs creating public art pieces for the Work Projects Administration (WPA).

The WPA had artists paint larger-than-life **murals** in public buildings such as post offices to remind people of good times and to give them hope. José Moya del Pino created several murals in California. Inside the Aztec Bakery in San Diego, he painted colorful murals of Mexican flowers and animals. Other murals showed scenes from Aztec life.

José Clemente Orozco lived in the United States from 1927 to 1934. His fresco, *Prometheus*, created for Pomona College in California, was the first mural painted by a Mexican in the United States.

The Mexican painter Diego Rivera worked in the United States during the Great Depression and inspired many Hispanic artists. His brightly colored murals pictured

Man at the Crossroads, 1934, by Diego Rivera. After the mural in Rockefeller Center was destroyed, Rivera recreated the painting in Mexico City.

people in scenes from Mexican life, politics, and history. In New York City's Rockefeller Center, Rivera painted a mural of workers at the crossroads of capitalism and socialism, science and industry. The painting was destroyed, however, because it included a portrait of Vladimir Lenin, a Russian revolutionary and the first Soviet leader. Rivera never worked in the United States again.

Magdalena Carmen Frida Kahlo y Calderón, better known as Frida Kahlo, was born in a small town near Mexico City. She is considered one of the greatest woman artists of all time. Many of her paintings are self-portraits or have female themes. Kahlo struggled with severe pain from a childhood accident all her life. Known for their dreamlike quality, her paintings often featured images of pain.

Self-Portrait with Changuito, 1945, by Frida Kahlo

On December 7, 1941, the Japanese bombed Pearl Harbor in Hawaii, and shortly afterward, the United States entered World War II. To send information about the war back home to the public, the army hired painters to be official war artists. Carlos Lopez came to the United States with his parents at age 11. He was already well known for his paintings and murals when he was hired by the U.S. Department of War. Lopez traveled with the Army in Europe, and later he painted Navy training activities.

There were several military bases in southern California, and servicemen on weekend leave often headed for Los Angeles. They wandered the city, looking for a good time. On May 30, 1943, a dozen servicemen started toward a group of young Hispanic women. To reach them, they had to pass several *pachucos*. These Hispanic boys were dressed in oversized jackets with broad shoulders and baggy balloon-like pants called "zoot suits," a style they'd picked up from young

Concrete Ship Side, ca. 1943, by Carlos Lopez.
In this painting, sailors practice bringing their landing craft alongside a concrete model of the side of a ship.

Soldiers and sailors roam the streets of Los Angeles armed with wooden clubs during the Zoot Suit Riots.

African Americans. One of the sailors grabbed the arm of a *pachuco* and a fight started. The *pachucos* won and the servicemen left—but not for long.

A few days later, about 50 sailors carrying bats and other weapons went looking for *pachucos*. In a theater they found some 12- and 13-year-olds wearing zoot suits. The sailors beat the boys and ripped off their clothes and burned them. The rioting went on for more than a week, with servicemen prowling Hispanic neighborhoods looking for zoot-suiters.

On June 7, a newspaper printed a guide on how to "de-zoot" a *pachuco*. Several thousand people were in the mob that night. Many Mexican Americans were arrested, but no charges were filed against the soldiers and sailors. Finally, Los Angeles was declared off-limits to servicemen, and the riots ended. Afterward, zoot suits were outlawed in the city. The Zoot Suit Riots inspired many Hispanic artists, who later created songs, poems, paintings, and murals about the tragedy.

Tito Puente was the first to use the timbal, a double drum played with sticks, in his music.

After the Spanish-American War ended in 1898, Puerto Rico became a United States possession. In 1917, its people were granted citizenship. Though they could not vote, they could move freely between their island and the States. By the 1930s, there were roughly 40,000 Puerto Ricans living on the mainland. After World War II ended, thousands more arrived in search of good jobs. In just one year, between 1945 and 1946, the number of Puerto Ricans in New York City went from about 13,000 to 50,000. Most settled in a Manhattan neighborhood that became known as Spanish Harlem.

In 1923, the "King of Latin Music" was born in Spanish Harlem. Ernesto Anthony "Tito" Puente grew up to play the piano, timbales, and other musical instruments, lead bands, and write hundreds of musical pieces. After his album, the 1958 *Dance Mania*, was released, a Latin American dance known as the mambo became popular. Puente received four Grammy Awards for his work, which has inspired many other Hispanic musicians.

People of Puerto Rican descent also contributed to the New York art scene. Joseph Rodríguez was born in Brooklyn in 1951. He became a photographer while in his 30s and has since won many awards. Rodríguez has also published several books, including *Spanish Harlem* and *East Side Stories: Gang Life in East L.A.* Both books picture people's struggle to live their lives amid poverty and violence.

Puerto Rican Flag, 1986, by Joseph Rodríguez.
In a poor area of Spanish Harlem, a Puerto Rican flag creates a bright spot in a boarded-up storefront.

Born in 1751, José Campeche is considered Puerto Rico's first important painter. His mother was Spanish and his father was a freed slave. Campeche first learned painting from his father, a self-taught artist. Later, he studied with Luis Paret Alcázar, a painter who had been banished from Spain. Campeche created about 400 portraits and paintings of religious subjects. Shown is *Don José Mas Ferrer*, which was painted about 1795.

31

MAGICAL REALISM

Gabriel García Márquez (left) left the United States after receiving death threats because he supported Fidel Castro (right) and communist Cuba. The two men remain friends today.

The term *magical realism* was invented in 1925 by Franz Roh, a German. He used it to describe the dreamlike work of a group of artists who included both magical and real things in their work. By the 1940s, magical realism came to describe the stories of Latin American writers. Like the painters, these authors wrote stories that blended magical and dreamlike happenings. Often, they used material based on myths or fairytales.

Colombian-born Gabriel García Márquez was one of the greatest writers of magical realism. In his stories, flowers sometimes fall from the sky instead of rain. Marquez moved his family to New York City in 1959 but only stayed for a year before moving to Mexico. His best known novel is *100 Years of Solitude*. Published in 1967, it traces the history of one family in a magical town. In 1982, Márquez received the Nobel Prize in Literature for his work.

Persistence of Memory, 1931, by Salvador Dali (right, in 1954)

Isabel Allende is also known for magical realism. She lived in Chile but fled after her uncle's government was overthrown in 1973. One of her most famous works, *The House of the Spirits*, is loosely based on her family's history. Today, Allende writes and teaches in the United States.

The painters' form of magical realism is now called **surrealism**. Spanish-born Salvador Dali is one of the most famous surrealists. In 1940, Dali moved to New York City to escape World War II. There he designed clothes for Coco Chanel and continued to paint. He also worked with director Alfred Hitchcock on the film *Spellbound*, which was released in 1945. Dali designed a scary, dreamlike scene that includes floating eyeballs and a man without a face.

Cuban rebel leader Fidel Castro (seated) with two armed followers at their Sierra Maestra mountain hideout in eastern Cuba

In 1959, Fidel Castro and his Communist Party took over the island country of Cuba. By the time air service was stopped in 1962, about 200,000 people had fled to the United States. Between 1965 and 1973, flights were once again allowed, bringing about 300,000 more. For about six months in 1980, Cubans were allowed to leave from the port of Mariel. With the help of Americans, about 125,000 of them arrived in Florida.

Most Cubans settled in Miami in a neighborhood that would come to be called Little Havana, after Cuba's capital city. Many of them had not been able to bring all their belongings, but they did bring their memories of Cuba, its stories, songs, dances, and artistic traditions. Cuban music echoed through the streets of Little Havana, and the smell of Cuban foods filled the air.

Paul Sierra was 16 years old when he left Cuba for Miami with his family in 1961. Shortly afterward, they moved to Chicago where Sierra studied at the School of the Art Institute of Chicago. His colorful paintings often include elements of magical realism.

Another World, 2002,
by Paul Sierra

Desiderio Alberto Arnaz II, a congressman in Cuba, was sent to prison when Fulgencio Batista took over the government in 1933. His wife fled to Miami with their son, Desi. Right after high school, young Desi Arnaz joined Xavier Cugat's band. By 1939, he was starring in a Broadway play. In 1940, Desi met and married Lucille Ball. *I Love Lucy*, the couple's hit TV series, began its run in 1951. Desi's performances on the show helped make Cuban music and dances, such as the conga, mambo, rumba, and cha-cha, popular throughout the United States.

CHAPTER 5

A GROWING INFLUENCE

César Chávez formed a union that helped workers get better pay and working conditions by using nonviolent means such as marches, boycotts, and strikes.

The 1960s were a time of great unrest in the United States. People marched to protest the Vietnam War. The Civil Rights Movement fought for equal rights for African Americans. Many Mexican Americans, or Chicanos, felt that they, too, were second-class citizens. Most of them had unskilled jobs and many families were poor. The Chicano Movement, also called the Mexican-American Civil Rights Movement, was born in the mid-1960s.

In New Mexico, Reies López Tijerina fought for Chicano lands lost after the Mexican-American War. In Colorado, Rodolfo "Corky" Gonzales started the Crusade for Justice to fight for Chicano rights and get more Chicanos involved in local government. His epic poem, "I Am Joaquin," came to stand for all Chicanos in America. César Chávez and Dolores Huerta fought for better pay and working conditions for Hispanics who worked on farms. In 1962, they founded

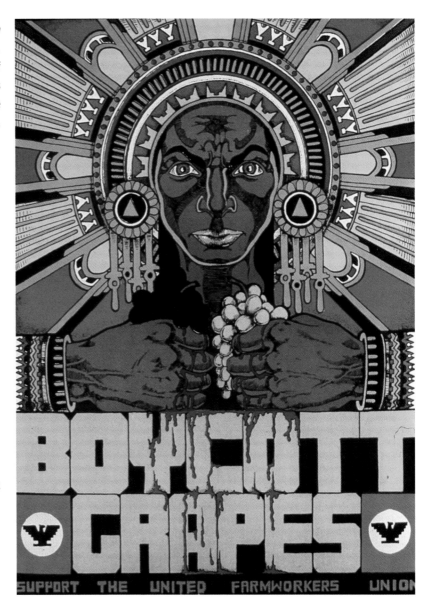

Boycott Grapes: Support the United Farm Workers Union, 1973, Xavier Viramontes. Viramontes made the poster in support of the farm workers' struggle for fair wages and working conditions. He used a godlike Aztec image to create a strong impact.

the National Farm Workers Association, which later became the United Farm Workers Union.

Much Hispanic art during this time encouraged social change and often pictured the hard lives of poor, working-class Hispanics. The earliest artworks were created for the United Farm Workers. Colorful posters asked people to support the workers by not buying certain products, such as lettuce or grapes.

To bring art to the people, many artists drew posters and flyers, which could be cheaply produced. Rupert García helped lead the Chicano Art Movement. He formed civil rights groups that held protests against the poor treatment of Hispanics. García started the San Francisco Poster Workshop. He drew one of its most famous posters, a portrait of Che Guevara, a Latin American doctor turned revolutionary.

At the same time, writers started new Hispanic magazines and newspapers. The most famous was *Caracol*, a national magazine edited by Cecilio García-Camarillo and based in San Antonio, Texas.

One goal of Hispanic writers was to celebrate the Spanish language. They felt that Spanish should be as accepted in the United States as English. Some Hispanic writers' books were bilingual, written in both Spanish and English. The authors switched between languages, depending on what they were writing about. A sentence could begin in English, switch to Spanish in the middle,

Artist Rupert García in 1997

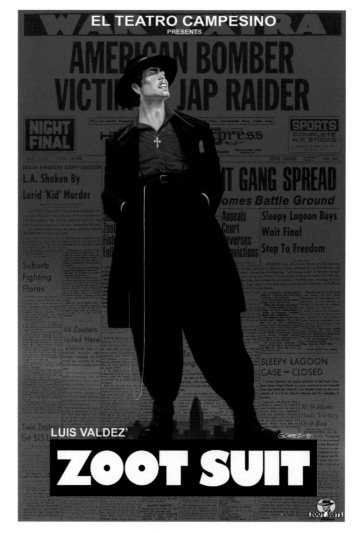

Luis Valdez's play *Zoot Suit*, about the Zoot Suit Riots, opened in Los Angeles in 1978.

and then back to English. The term *Spanglish* was coined to describe this mix of Spanish and English.

Angela de Hoyos was born in Mexico but moved with her family to San Antonio, Texas, when still a child. Her 1975 book of poetry, *Arise Chicano! and Other Poems,* was inspired by the struggle of the United Farm Workers. De Hoyos often uses Spanglish in her poetry. Many of her more recent poems are about women and their lives.

Playwright Luis Valdez was one of the leaders of the Chicano Theater Movement. In 1965, he founded El Teatro Campesino, a traveling group of actors who performed plays for farm workers. He also wrote plays. Inspired by Valdez's work, small Chicano theaters sprang up in many cities throughout the United States.

The Chicano Movement opened many doors for talented Hispanics. Musicians in the 1970s and 1980s recorded new songs that blended Hispanic music and other types of music, such as pop and rock. Singer and songwriter Gloria Estefan was born in Cuba, but her parents brought her to Miami when she was just one year old. She taught herself to play guitar by listening to the radio. Some of her songs, such as "Conga," feature Latin dances. Others are written in Spanglish and celebrate Cuban culture.

Carlos Santana's 38 albums showcase his expert guitar playing.

Carlos Santana's music blends African and Hispanic rhythms with blues and rock. In 1998, he and his band Santana earned a placed in the Rock and Roll Hall of Fame, and in 1999 their album *Supernatural* won nine Grammy Awards. In 2005, Santana, accompanied by Spanish actor Antonio Banderas, performed *"Al Otro Lado del Rio"* at the Academy Awards ceremony. Written by Jorge Drexler of Uruguay, the song was the first one written and sung in Spanish to win an Academy Award.

Music, 2005, Xavier Cortada

In 1989, Oscar Hijuelos became the first Hispanic author to win a Pulitzer Prize for fiction for *The Mambo Kings Play Songs of Love*. The book describes the Cuban music scene of the 1950s and was made into a movie in 1992.

Xavier Cortada is a Cuban-American artist who organizes community art projects. He creates mosaics and pictures, but he specializes in murals that express the experiences of different ethnic peoples in the United States. Cortada's *Stepping into the American Dream* was the official mural for The White House Conference on Minority Homeownership in 2002.

Many consider Puerto Rican Roberto Clemente one of the greatest baseball players of all time. He earned many awards, including 12 Gold Glove awards for his outfield skill. Sadly, Clemente died at age 38, soon after reaching an amazing 3,000 career hits. His plane crashed in 1972 while he was flying supplies to earthquake victims in Nicaragua. Clemente was voted into the National Baseball Hall of Fame in 1973.

Judy Baca is both an artist and a community leader in Los Angeles. Baca's large, colorful murals explore what it means to be a woman and Hispanic. In 1974, Baca started the Los Angeles mural program, which helped keep gang members from fighting by having them work together to create art.

Baca also founded SPARC (the Social and Public Arts Resource Center) in Venice, California. Her first SPARC project in 1976 was *The Great Wall of Los Angeles*. This half-mile-long mural pictures scenes from California's history. It took five years and the help of about 400 teenagers and 50 other artists to complete the mural.

Richard Serra is best known for his large sculptures made of steel, lead, and other industrial materials. The parts of his "prop

The Matter of Time, 2005, Richard Serra. In May 2005, Serra's work, which consists of seven huge sculptures, was installed in the Guggenheim Museum in Bilbao, Spain.

El Chandelier, by Pepón Osorio, 1988. Chandeliers are found in many apartments in Spanish Harlem. Osorio created this one out of mass-produced pop-culture items from the 1950s and 1960s, when many Puerto Ricans left their island for New York.

pieces" are not attached, but held in place by weight and gravity. In 1981, he installed *Tilted Arc*, a 120-foot- (36.5-m-) long, 12-foot- (3.6-m-) high curved steel wall at Federal Plaza in New York City. Many people who worked there didn't like it. Talk of removing it led Serra to file a lawsuit, but the courts ruled against him, and the sculpture was destroyed in 1989.

Pepón Osorio is also a sculptor, but of a very different kind. Instead of using heavy metals, he assembles his artworks from knickknacks, such as plastic dolls and other mass-produced objects. Many of his works refer back to his days as a social worker in the Bronx and Spanish Harlem.

The work of Hispanics can be seen in major museums as well as museums that specialize in Hispanic art, such as El Museo del Barrio in New York City. There are Spanish-language newspapers, magazines, and television stations. Hispanic musicians and actors star in TV shows and feature films. Teenagers all over the country dance to the beat of salsa music. Today, Hispanic arts and culture are more vital than ever before.

1492 Christopher Columbus crosses the Atlantic to Hispaniola

1519 Hernán Cortés and his army arrive in Mexico

1540 Francisco Vasquez de Coronado sets out to find Cíbola

1557 First painters' guild established in Mexico City

1566 Simón Pereyns (d. 1589) arrives in Mexico

1568 Andrés de la Concha (d. 1612) arrives in Mexico

ca. 1558 Baltásar de Echave Orio born (d. ca. 1623), arrives in Mexico 1582

ca. 1585 Luis Juárez born (d. 1639)

1562 Construction begins on Metropolitan Cathedral in Mexico City (ends 1813)

1565 The Spanish conquer the Philippines

1598 Juan de Oñate founds first Spanish colony in New Mexico

early 1600s First Spanish missions built in Arizona

1609 Baltásar de Echave Orio starts first art school for Spanish students born in New Spain

1636 Antonio Rodríguez born (d. 1691)

ca. 1650 Sor Juana Inés de la Cruz born (d. 1695)

1682 First Spanish missions built in Texas

ca. 1695 Miguel Cabrera born (d. 1768)

1700s *Casta* paintings become popular in New Spain

1746 Luis Paret Alcázar born (d. 1799)

mid-1700s First Spanish missions built in California

1752 José Campeche born (d. 1809)

1767 Junípero Serra is put in charge of building missions in California

mid- to late 1700s *Enconchados* develop as an art form

1787–1803 Martin de Sessé y Lacasta and José Mariano Mociño explore from Central America north to Alaska

1810 Mexican Revolutionary War begins (ends 1821)

1835 Texas Revolution begins (ends 1836)

1836 Mexican soldiers under Antonio López de Santa Anna defeat Americans at the Alamo; Republic of Texas formed

1840 José María Velasco born (d. 1912)

1844 José María Apodaca born (d. 1924)

1845 Texas becomes a state

1846 Mexican-American War begins (ends 1848)

mid-1800s *Corridos* become popular

1851 José Guadalupe Posada born (d. 1913)

1876 Joseph Jacinto Mora born (d. 1947)

1883 José Clemente Orozco born (d. 1949)

1886 Diego Rivera born (d. 1957)

1898 Spanish-American War takes place

1900 Xavier Cugat born (d. 1990)

1904 Salvador Dali born (d. 1989)

1907 Frida Kahlo born (d. 1954)

1908 Carlos Lopez born (d. 1953)

1910 Mexican Revolution begins (ends 1920)

1917 People of Puerto Rico granted U.S. citizenship; Desi Arnaz born (d. 1986)

1923 Ernesto Anthony "Tito" Puente born (d. 2000)

1925 Term *magical realism* invented by Franz Roh

1928 Gabriel García Márquez born

1929 Great Depression begins (ends 1940)

1933 Fulgencio Batista takes over Cuban government

1934 Roberto Clemente born (d. 1972)

1939 World War II begins (ends 1945); Richard Serra born

1940 Angela de Hoyos born; Luis Valdez born

1941 United States enters World War II; Rupert Garcia born

1942 Isabel Allende born

1943 Zoot Suit Riots take place in Los Angeles, California; Xavier Viramontes born

1944 Paul Sierra born; Cecilio García-Camarillo born (d. 2002)

1946 Judy Baca born

1947 Carlos Santana born

1951 Joseph Rodríguez born; Oscar Hijuelos born

1955 Pepón Osorio born

1957 Gloria Estefan born

1959 Fidel Castro and Communist Party take over Cuba

1960 Antonio Banderas born

1962 National Farm Workers Association founded (becomes United Farm Workers Union in 1965)

1964 Xavier Cortada born; Jorge Drexler born

mid-1960s Mexican-American Civil Rights Movement born

1982 Gabriel García Márquez wins Nobel Prize in Literature

1989 Oscar Hijuelos becomes first Hispanic author to win Pulitzer Prize for fiction

adobe building material made of mud mixed with straw and then dried in the sun

apprentice a beginner who is working with a master in his or her field to learn a trade

baroque a style defined by highly detailed decoration

broadside a large sheet of paper, usually printed on one side and folded

bulto statue, usually of a religious figure

calacas pictures or sculptures of skeletons

calaveras pictures or sculptures of skulls

caste a social division based on differences in race

colcha an embroidery stitch; also the bed covering or other fabric decorated with *colcha* stitches

corrido a song that tells a story with a lesson

enconchado a picture that combines painting with mother-of-pearl insets

fresco the art of painting on fresh, moist plaster with pigments dissolved in water

guild a group of painters or other craftspeople

Hispanic of or relating to a Spanish-speaking people or culture; also a U.S. citizen or resident of Latin American or Spanish descent

inscription a caption on a painting

majolica pottery covered with a tin glaze and decorated with colored designs

marquetry a decorative art form in which patterns are formed by inlaying wood, stone, straw, or other materials into a sheet of wood

mission a church complex built to encourage Spanish settlement and convert native peoples to Catholicism

mural a very large image, such as a painting or an enlarged photograph, often applied directly to a wall or ceiling

retablo an altar screen in a church

santero an artist who creates religious images such as *bultos*

surrealism a type of painting that includes dreamlike or fantastic elements

vaquero a Mexican cowhand

The California Missions by Dale Anderson, World Almanac Library, 2002

Frida Kahlo: Portrait of a Mexican Painter (Hispanic Biographies) by Barbara Cruz, Enslow, 1996

Latino Arts and Their Influence on the United States: Songs, Dreams, and Dances (Hispanic Heritage) by Rory Makosz, Mason Crest Publishers, 2005

Latin Sensations (A&E Biography) by Heron Marquez, Lerner, 2001

The New York Public Library Amazing Hispanic American History: A Book of Answers for Kids (The New York Public Library Books for Kids) by George Ochoa, Wiley, 1998

Tito Puente (Hispanic-American Biographies) by Mary Olmstead, Raintree, 2004

Web Sites

Celebrate Hispanic Heritage

http://teacher.scholastic.com/activities/hispanic/index.htm

The Museum of Spanish Colonial Art: Information on the traditional arts

http://www.spanishcolonial.org/arts.shtml

SPARC Murals

www.sparcmurals.org

Smithsonian for Kids: A Puerto Rican Carnival. Includes how to make a carnival mask and links to other sites on Puerto Rican Culture

http://americanhistory2.si.edu/ourstoryinhistory/tryathome/activities_carnival.html

ACKNOWLEDGMENTS

The editors wish to thank the following organizations and individuals for permission to reprint the literary quotes and to reproduce the images in this book. Every effort has been made to obtain permission from the owners of all materials. Any errors that may have been made are unintentional and will be corrected in future printings if notice is given to the publisher.

Cover: José Agustin Arrieta/*Market Place*, Mexico, 1850/Oil on canvas/The Art Archive/National History Museum, Mexico City/Dagli Orti

Title page, p. 11: Old Spanish mission church at Taos Pueblo, New Mexico/Library of Congress

Contents: Ablestock

p. 4: Columbus taking possession of the new country/Chromolithograph/Published 1893/Library of Congress

p. 5: *Portrait of Montezuma* (detail), between 1680 and 1697/Attributed to Antonio Rodríguez/Oil on canvas/The Art Archive/Palazzo Pitti, Florence/Dagli Orti

p. 6: Quetzal-feather headdress said to belong to Montezuma/The Art Archive/Museum für Völkerkunde, Vienna/Dagli Orti

p. 7 (top): Iuanes Cuiris/*Maria*/Feather mosaic/SK Kap 322/Kunsthistorisches Museum, Wien oder KHM, Wien; **(bottom):** Coronado's March, Colorado, ca. 1897/Library of Congress

p. 8: Luis Juárez/*The Guardian Angel*/The Art Archive/Pinacoteca Virreinel, Mexico City/Dagli Orti

p. 9 (top): *Festival in an Indian Village*, between 1650 and 1700/Unknown artist/10-panel folding screen/Oil on canvas/The Art Archive; **(bottom):** Miguel Cabrera/*Portrait of Sor Juana Inés de la Cruz*, 1750/The Art Archive/National History Museum, Mexico City/Dagli Orti

p. 10: Metropolitan Cathedral, Mexico City/The Art Archive/Dagli Orti

p. 11 (top): *Retablo*, 17th century/Santo Domingo Church, Oaxaca, Mexico/The Art Archive/Dagli Orti

p. 12: *Portrait of an Indian Noblewoman: Sebastian Inés Josefa de San Agustín*, 1757/Unknown artist/The Art Archive/Museo Franz Mayer, Mexico/Dagli Orti

p. 13 (top): *Casta* painting: *Alvarazado* man, mulatto woman, and *borquino* child, 18th century/Unknown artist/The Art Archive/Rodolfo Gonzalez Garza Collection, Monterrey/Dagli Orti; **(bottom):** Watercolor of *Lobelia cardinalis subsp. graminea* (Lam.) McVaugh, Hunt Institution accession 6331.1359/Courtesy of Hunt Institute for Botanical Documentation, Carnegie Mellon University, Pittsburgh, PA, Torner Collection of Sessé and Mociño Biological Illustrations

p. 14: Wool on wool *colcha*, late 18th–19th century, New Mexico/Museum of Spanish Colonial Art/Collections of the Spanish Colonial Arts Society, Inc. Photo by Jack Parsons/1957.41

p. 15 (top): Rio Grande blanket, ca. 1900, New Mexico/Museum of Spanish Colonial Art/Collections of the Spanish Colonial Arts Society, Inc. Photo by Jack Parsons/1969.15; **(bottom):** Statue of Father Junípero Serra/Copyright © North Wind/Nancy Carter/North Wind Picture Archives/All rights reserved

p. 16: Santa Fe Federal/Neoclassical style tin frame with lithograph of Christ Child of Atocha, ca. 1840–1870, New Mexico. Print by Cabrera of Calle Tacuba, Mexico City/Museum of Spanish Colonial Art/Collections of the Spanish Colonial Arts Society, Inc. Photo by Jack Parsons/1956.39

p. 17 (top): Straw appliqué box, 19th century, Mexico/Museum of Spanish Colonial Art/Collections of the Spanish Colonial Arts Society, Inc. Photo by Jack Parsons/1990.80; **(bottom):** San Juan Bautista (St. John the Baptist) *santo*, 19th century, Mexico/ Colonial Arts, San Francisco, CA

p. 18: Aztec skull mask with flint-knife nose/The Art Archive/Museo del Templo Mayor, Mexico/Dagli Orti

p. 19 (top): José Guadalupe Posada/*Gran calavera eléctrica*/Library of Congress; **(bottom):** Ceremonial mask, Mexico/The Art Archive/Mask Museum, San Luis Potosi, Mexico/Mireille Vautier

p. 20: A. Serrano/*Miguel Hidalgo y Costilla*/The Art Archive/National History Museum, Mexico City/Dagli Orti

p. 21: José María Velasco/*Valley of Mexico Seen from the Heights of Tacubaya*/The Art Archive/Museum of Modern Art, Mexico/Dagli Orti

p. 22: *Antonio López de Santa Anna*/Unknown artist/The Art Archive/National History Museum, Mexico City/Dagli Orti

p. 23: Mexican vaquero, ca. 1890/The Art Archive/Bill Manns

p. 24: Excerpt from "*El corrido de Kiansis*" Courtesy Manuel Peña and UCLA Chicano Studies Research Center; "Corrido de la Cucaracha," published 1915/Illustration by José Guadalupe Posada/Library of Congress

p. 25: Pancho (Francesco) Villa, Emiliano Zapata, and fellow revolutionaries in the presidential salon, 1911/The Art Archive/National History Museum, Mexico City/Dagli Orti

p. 26: Frida Kahlo and Diego Rivera, 1932/Carl Van Vechten, photographer/Library of Congress

p. 27 (top): Diego Rivera/*Man at the Crossroads*, 1934/Fresco/The Art Archive/Museo del Palacio de Bellas Artes, Mexico/Dagli Orti/Instituto Nacional de Bellas Artes/© 2005 Banco de México Diego Rivera & Frida Kahlo Museums Trust. Av. Cinco de Mayo No. 2, Col. Centro, Del. Cuauhtémoc 06059, México, D.F.; **(bottom):** Frida Kahlo/Self-Portrait with Changuito/The Art Archive/Dolores Olmedo, Mexico/Dagli Orti/Dagli Orti/Instituto Nacional de Bellas Artes/© 2005 Banco de México Diego Rivera & Frida Kahlo Museums Trust. Av. Cinco de Mayo No. 2, Col. Centro, Del. Cuauhtémoc 06059, México, D.F.

p. 28: Carlos Lopez/*Concrete Ship Side*, ca. 1943/Oil on canvas/Gift of Abbott Laboratories/Naval Historical Foundation/88-159-HE

p. 29: U.S. armed forces personnel with wooden clubs during Zoot Suit Riots in Los Angeles, 1943/Library of Congress

p. 30: Tito Puente/Fandango/Canal +/-SGAE/The Kobal Collection/Socias, Jordi

p. 31 (top): Joseph Rodríguez (1951–)/*Puerto Rican Flag*, 1986/Chromogenic photograph on paper, 12 x 18 in (30.5 x 45.7 cm)/Gift of the artist/Smithsonian American Art Museum, Washington, DC/Art Resource, NY; **(bottom):** José Campeche y Jordan (1751–1809)/*Don José Mas Ferrer*, ca. 1795/Oil/21 1/4 x 16 3/8 in./Teodoro Vidal Collection/Smithsonian American Art Museum, Washington, DC/Art Resource, NY

p. 32: Gabriel García Márquez and Fidel Castro. 2002/Alejandro Ernesto/Notimex/Newscom

p. 33 (top): Salvador Dali/*Persistence of Memory*/1931/The Art Archive/Museum of Modern Art, New York/Joseph Martin/© 2005 Salvador Dali, Gala-Salvador Dali Foundation/Artists Rights Society (ARS), New York; **(bottom):** Salvador Dali, 1954/Carl Van Vechten, Photographer/Library of Congress

p. 34: Fidel Castro and two followers at Sierra Maestra mountain hideout, Cuba/Library of Congress

p. 35 (top): *Another World*, 2002/© Paul Sierra/Courtesy of the artist; **(bottom):** Lucille Ball and Desi Arnaz/MGM/The Kobal Collection/Bull, Clarence Sinclair

p. 36: César Chávez during grape boycott, 1984/Photographer Showcase/Copyright David Bacon/Newscom

p. 37: *Boycott Grapes: Support the United Farm Workers Union*, 1973/© Xavier Viramontes/Courtesy of the artist

p. 38: "Tamalada" by Angela de Hoyos is reprinted with permission from the publisher of *Chicano Poems: for the Barrio* (M&A Editions, 1975 and Arte Público Press— University of Houston.); Rupert Garcia/Photo © David Bacon

p. 39: *Zoot Suit* written by Luis Valdez/Artwork by Ignacio Gomez/Courtesy of El Teatro Campesino

p. 40: Carlos Santana/2005/Luis Moreno/Notimex/Newscom

p. 41 (top): *Music* (acrylic on canvas) by Xavier Cortada (b. 1964)/Private Collection/Bridgeman Art Library; **(bottom):** Roberto Clemente, 1970/Malcolm Emmons-US PRESSWIRE/Zuma Press/Larry W. Smith/Icon SMI/Newscom

p. 42: Richard Serra/*The Matter of Time*, 2005/Guggenheim Museum, Bilbao, Spain/Luis Tejido/EPA Photos/Newscom

p. 43: Pepón Osorio (b. 1955)/*El Chandelier*, 1988/Functional metal and glass chandelier with plastic toys, figurines, glass crystals and objects/60 7/8 x 42" diam./© 1988 Pepón Osorio/Smithsonian American Art Museum/Art Resource, NY/Courtesy Ronald Feldman Fine Arts, New York

Backgrounds, pp. 4–5, 25, 35, 38, and all sidebar backgrounds: Ablestock

Backgrounds, pp. 6, 20, 22, 24, 36: Library of Congress